David Boyle is co-director of the New Weather Institute and the author of a range of books including *Broke: How to Survive the Middle Class Crisis, The Tyranny of Numbers* and *Authenticity*. He was the Government's independent reviewer for the Barriers to Choice Review in 2012/13 for the Treasury and the Cabinet Office.

Tony Greenham is a former banker who is now head of Finance and Business at the New Economics Foundation, and author of a number of publications on banking reform. He sits on the advisory panel of the Government's Regional Growth Fund.

Friends Provident Foundation is an independent grant-making charity working to support greater economic resilience through building knowledge and taking action at the strategic and local levels. It is particularly interested in supporting the development of economic and financial systems that are designed to include those who are most vulnerable to market failure. For more information go to www.friendsprovidentfoundation.org.

The New Weather Institute is a mutual think-tank dedicated to changing the intellectual weather with new thinking, new ideas and new debate.

PEOPLE POWERED PROSPERITY

PEOPLE POWERED PROSPERITY

ULTRA-LOCAL APPROACHES TO MAKING POORER PLACES WEALTHIER

David Boyle and Tony Greenham

New Weather Institute

Ultra-local approaches to making poorer places wealthier

First edition published in paperback in Great Britain in 2015

The New Weather Institute
http://www.newweather.org

The moral right of David Boyle and Tony Greenham to be identified as the authors of this work has been asserted by them in accordance with the Copyright, Designs and Patents Acts of 1988.

Every effort has been made to trace or contact all copyright holders. The publishers will be pleased to make good any omissions or rectify any mistakes brought to their attention at the earliest opportunity. No responsibility can be accepted by the publisher for action taken as a result of information contained in this publication.

A CIP catalogue record for this book is available from the British Library.

ISBN: 978-0-9926919-4-3 (print)
ISBN: 978-0-992691-5-0 (ePub)

The New Weather Institute supports The Forest Stewardship Council [FSC], the leading international forest certification organization. All New Weather Institute titles are printed on FSC certified paper.

Project Managed by EDDEPRO Services 01548 858963
Cover illustration www.joshuabrent.com
Cover design and art direction www.danfarleydesign.co.uk
Typeset by www.hewertext.com

Printed and bound in Great Britain by Russell Press Limited, Nottingham NG6 0BT

Contents

Foreword by the Rt Hon Danny Alexander MP
Chief Secretary to the Treasury

I am in the privileged position of being able to influence our national economy from within the heart of the Government as Chief Secretary to the Treasury, and at the same time being able to see how national and local economic factors combine on the ground through my role as the Member of Parliament for Inverness, Nairn, Badenoch and Strathspey. My liberal instinct, and the fact that I grew up in a small island community, has given me a strong sense that we should always encourage beneficial local and community initiatives, economic or otherwise.

By doing so, we help ensure that every community in the nation can hold their head high with dignity and a degree of independence from Whitehall. Giving people the levers to affect their own locality in the form of an economic toolbox could also be a vital element in devolving more power to the cities, regions and nations of the UK, as we must do.

The difficulty is that such local levers are only in their earliest stages of development. I have been enormously impressed with the energy and dedication of the emerging community bankers and community energy pioneers who are making such a difference where they live. As just one example, I've spent Bristol pounds on a recent visit to that city. I've done everything I can to encourage communication between central government policy-makers and these innovators, aware that there are practical barriers and conceptual disagreements that are still hindering their new techniques.

So I am delighted that David Boyle and his colleagues at New Weather have carved out the space and time to tackle this issue – to pin down the disagreements, to look ahead at what might be possible, to translate the different participants to each other. I might not agree with every word. I might not nod at the logic of every argument, but I am extremely pleased that this report has been researched and believe the authors have done us a service peering into the future to see if there are better ways forward. I believe that, in this respect, they are right.

That makes this an important and timely investigation. I am very pleased to have helped to bring it about, and even more pleased that it has reached such an encouraging and positive fruition.

Danny Alexander

1.   Introduction

Can we find economic techniques which cities can use effectively to tackle their own market failures – and release their own wasted economic potential – and if so, why hasn't this happened already?

Some places use their land effectively and productively, and their people too. Those who want to do paid work can find it, and they get paid enough to support the kind of shops and facilities they want. Some places don't enjoy these skills and advantages, leaving swathes of the population jobless and swathes of the land full of weeds.

This is the economic problem at a local level, and it is an important one – not just here, but everywhere in the world. It governs politics and administrative structures. It is the justification for centralised systems of redistribution and other inconvenient speed bumps for local development – and it tends to become a vicious circle. The poor places get poorer, they become more dependent, and increasingly live off grants from central government and the hope of external investment that never comes.

Occasionally they are regenerated and outside money pours in to snap up the cheap land. Luxury yachts appear in new marinas. The property prices rise and the poor people move elsewhere. This is not really a solution.

But what if mainstream economic policy entrenched this vicious spiral, because it ignored some of the tools that places needed to regenerate themselves – to create a local prosperity primarily using the resources which they already have at their disposal. Because, even if it doesn't actually entrench the problem, the attitude of mainstream economic policy-makers tends to be a bit confused. They tend to concentrate on the places that can provide the best return. They tend to hand over the struggling places with spare capacity, not to economic specialists, but to welfare ones.

This is the peculiarity about mainstream policy when it comes to local revival. Everywhere is one thing or the other, black or white: either it is an economic problem or it is a welfare one, either worthy of investment or worthy of welfare support. This selective approach fails to take into account all the factors at play and therefore fails to treat the problem in its entirety. There appears to be no integration.

Of course, there is a bundle of policies which purport to do this – economic policy-makers traditionally fall back, the more local they get, on building things: marinas, shopping centres, roads, railway links. This is really neither economic policy nor welfare policy; it is land use policy, based on the idea that economic activity will follow. It is not what economic policy is about at national level – the flow of money around the national economy – and there appears to be little parallel interest about how money flows around a *local* economy.

This book is an investigation into the absence of this integrated approach and what might be done about it. People-Powered Prosperity digs down among the wasted resources to explore the local level where the economic levers are ignored, when they could be manipulated to release the wasted economic potential and ingenuity, giving entire communities the means to make their lives better.

The great divide

The absence of a coherent alternative to treating areas as either economic or welfare problems, is a serious issue. It means that whole cities, especially in the old industrial regions of the UK, have been left without the means to support themselves, dependent on central government support which is increasingly being withdrawn when they are unlikely in the medium term to attract external investment because they cannot specialise. There are also few intermediaries which can support recovery from much nearer than London. There are intermediaries, Local Enterprise Partnerships (LEPs) now, but they are not yet the players they need to be.

Traditionally, there is also a nervousness about local economic data. You can't help feeling that, if the local economic problem was a business or an oil pipeline, or a disease, then the supporting data would have been delivered, allowing policy-makers to pay far closer attention to it. Where does the money actually go? How can we use it better in the seriously disadvantaged places? It is as if the more conservative economic policy-makers regard such an idea as heretical. The local economic problem has not been solved: it may not be solveable, but equally the tools may now be becoming available for us to try.

Might it be possible for any city, region or village, no matter how poor and hopeless, to find some of the some basic raw materials within themselves, bringing together the tools and what local energy remains, to claw back some measure of independence and set themselves on the path to prosperity? If this turned out to be possible, it would make an enormous difference, not just to the structure of UK Government, but to those corners of developed cities that remain desperate and dependent – and possibly to the abject dependence of parts of the developing world too. It would mean that we had real tools available that could change people's lives – develop cities more inclusively, cut welfare and increase the prosperity of the poorest places. And, by so doing, of the nation as a whole.

It could change everything. But is it possible?

The idea of ultra local economic regeneration is potentially so important that some of those techniques are beginning to emerge, wherever city leaders are attracting innovative and inspirational individuals to take up the roles. Perhaps most impressively, this is happening in America (North and South) and, to a lesser extent, in the UK. These are very early stages; the evidence is not there yet – nor really have the techniques been developed at any level of sophistication. But there is one obstacle that sits above all others: mainstream economic policy-makers do not recognise this as either possible or important.

They don't recognise it because of a fundamental

difference that underpins everything else. It is widely recognised that the UK is too centralised to function as effectively as it could. This results in administrative solutions that are not tailored to local needs and local imagination and ability remains subservient to the centre. It is not yet agreed that there is an important economic component to this centralisation. Advocates of ultra-local economics – what we call People-Powered Prosperity - propose that economic policy is too centralised to be effective in less advantaged areas, *and* economic institutions are too centralised to act effectively where they are needed most. This means that banking and investment are much too centralised, and therefore lack the information they need to be effective. But for some reason these issues have not yet made their way to the forefront of debate in the UK, as they have for example in the USA.

This short book is designed to find out why, and to translate two very different worlds to each other – the world of the Treasury economists and the world of the community bankers, community energy developers, local currency experimenters, and other local regenerators, who believe that they are on their way to cracking the local economic problem.

Writing *People-Powered Prosperity* involved interviews with a range of prominent economists and policy-makers and we are hugely grateful for the time they gave so freely to wrestle with these problems. We blame nobody for the situation – it is a symptom of the growing awareness of just how little there is, once you do the evaluations, in the conventional regeneration tool kit. Our project is a concerted attempt to go beyond that impasse and look ahead, in the hope that we can develop a shared way forward to provide places with the economic tools they need to help lift themselves up and out of dependency.

2. The regeneration paradox: people or places?

A number of issues about economic regeneration are getting in the way of innovation. They include:

- So much public policy is devoted to helping people leave impoverished areas, yet we know that most will not actually leave.
- The market anomalies are local but the levers remain national, and therefore imperfect.
- The ultra-local – or ultra-small approach to local regeneration – lacks a generally accepted or recognised name.

Bradford is one of the great cities of England. It grew twenty times over in the nineteenth century and became the centre of the spinning and woollen industries. The Independent Labour Party was born there. A century ago it was the centre of European Jewish culture, had three daily newspapers, orchestras and the theatre where Sir Henry Irving performed for the last time.

When J. B. Priestley visited there in 1933, having left the town originally at the outbreak of the First World War, he bemoaned the discovery that the German influence had gone and that the Theatre Royal had become a cinema "Wool merchants, whose names seemed to us like the Bank of England, have vanished. Not one or two of them, but dozens of them," he wrote in *English Journey*.[1]

Now, eight decades later, Bradford is a shadow even of this former self. The Otley Road area in particular is one of the most deprived communities in England, having a male life expectancy of just 70 years, seven years below the UK average. According to the Church Urban Fund, 36 per cent of children in Otley Road are living in poverty, as are 41 per cent of pensioners.[2] The food bank there covers the whole city, distributing 700 bags of food in May and June, up from 500 bags a month round about Christmas 2013.

This book is not about what happened to Bradford: the decades of poor decision-making, the failure of so many schemes – to make the city the heart of the media industry – and the development of Leeds next door as a major financial centre. The point is that Bradford was once an economic powerhouse, it isn't now and it isn't alone in this. Certainly not when you include the other junior partners of these linked cities across the Atlantic. For Bradford, the poor neighbour of Leeds, see also the desperate plight of Camden New Jersey on the other side of the river from Philadelphia, or East St Louis on the other side of the river from St Louis. The desperate places of the UK have not yet descended to those depths, but the basic pattern is the same.

The question is what we do about it.

But here the issue isn't quite so straightforward. The prevailing mainstream view is that it is the people of Bradford – for example – who need to be helped, even if they leave the city and move south. Of course, they do need support. But there is a policy view that dares not speak its name in public: that this is *all that can be achieved*. It is a quiet assent, partly because of the ferocious reaction to the 2008 Policy Exchange report *Cities Unlimited* which appeared to suggest giving up on regeneration attempts in Liverpool, Bradford, Sunderland and Hull, abandoning the cities to permanent economic decline – and, instead, focusing on investment programmes in the economically booming areas of the south of England.[3]

Of course, it would caricature both the report author, Dr Tim Leunig, and his subtle message, to suggest that he wanted to abandon northern cities like Bradford. But there is a logical position here which regards itself as being at odds with the practical orthodoxy, which is to keep the people of Bradford alive as dependent subjects of central government. Or when those funds run out, to hope that Local Enterprise Partnerships (LEPs), or some other combination of business know-how and infrastructure, will make a difference. This approach is also problematic: there is little evidence that this is effective, or that the new road and rail links don't just help business and investors to bypass places like Bradford even faster.

This is the great paradox of regeneration and it runs deep. Economic orthodoxy suggests that there is a way out for impoverished places: specialise, attract investment accordingly and trade your way out. But this also involves serious difficulties for places like Bradford, given the extreme centralisation of business in the UK. What would their specialisation be, either nationally or in an increasingly globalised economy, internationally? Should they even try to to replace their imports with their own products – what investment is available to them to do so?

This orthodoxy also works on the assumption that Bradford has no assets, yet this is far from clear. In particular, there is a wealth of talented women living in the suburbs, many of whom have given up careers to raise families, and who would – given the right sparks, conditions, support, opportunities and with the support of the right institutions – transform their neighbourhoods. These 'assets' are not picked up by any of the conventional measures, but they do represent the most intractable implications of the debate about regeneration.

Paradox 1: People don't leave

This is the difficulty for Bradford and those places like them, caught between regeneration orthodoxy (build infrastructure) and the new, unspoken economic orthodoxy (educate and train until people leave); it has left places like this with a disastrous paradox.

We know most people won't leave – even if, in a perfect economic world, they might like to – and not because they lack ambition, but for a host of other reasons. Nor should we want the kind of entirely rootless society where people *have* to leave, given the networks of informal support that keep them alive if they stay put. Similarly, an adverse effect of increased migration from north to south would also come through the impact of increased widening disparity in house prices.

This gap between theory and reality is a major block to progress. One of the problems with controlling all economic judgements from Whitehall is that, sometimes, theory wins over practice. Ideological solutions might require, for example, disparities in regional earnings that are not going to be socially acceptable and are therefore never going to happen. Yet these old theories can sometimes get in the way of more choice at local level.[4]

Paradox 2: Local problems, national levers

But there is another damaging paradox. In practice, economic policy-makers clearly can't abandon the struggling places, and the people who live there, to their fate. Yet they have not developed the proven economic techniques that can harness the data to support the development of enterprise locally, which would facilitate people's imagination and talents, enabling them to power their own prosperity. Yet these techniques work elsewhere in the world and there is evidence of their effectiveness.[5]

This failure to develop these here matters for a whole range of reasons, but three in particular.

- **It matters socially.** It means a rise in poverty and dependence, perhaps beyond what would have happened anyway.
- **It matters politically.** It means that there is

disaffection in the less successful places, which can turn rapidly into intolerance.

- **It also matters institutionally.** Policy-makers have not focused on what they need to do to make local economies work more effectively, and that means the institutions they set up to support enterprise will not always suit these areas.

This last one matters a great deal. It means, as a result, that there are institutions suited to dealing with big, national partners, rather than local institutions with local knowledge. Even if the entrepreneurial drive was there, the danger is that the regeneration institutions will not be able to find and facilitate it.

Paradox 3: The trouble with names

Any policy which labels itself 'local' is bound to be difficult for policy-makers (see overleaf). 'Community' economics avoids that particular worry, but instead implies we should emphasise the importance of supporting communities to take part in their local economy, to have greater control over assets, to be active in local decision-making and to foster a local enterprise culture. All of these processes can lead to economic outcomes which benefit local communities, but they don't necessarily lead to better economic outcomes just because more people are taking part – especially if the people then move away. In the same way, only focussing on improving the local economy might not support improved participation either.

Community economics *is* about building capacity but it

isn't directly about economics. And if there is a bundle of economic techniques which provide cities, towns or regions with economic levers, then it still lacks a name and it also lacks an effective description. As things stand, it's just a bundle of stories. That is how we will describe it in the next chapter.

3. Misunderstandings about regeneration

There are particular failures of communication which confuse things and prevent effective debate. These include:

- An unresolved debate about regeneration – how much by specialisation to earn more from outside? How much by replacing imports? How much by narrowing production and how much by shaping a diverse hinterland?
- The language of 'local' can get in the way, especially as what we are really talking about here is not really local, it is small.
- The mainstream is sceptical about the full value of the additionality – believing that all regeneration is usually just shifted from elsewhere.

Lessons from overseas

The economic plight of Quebec in the run-up to the hard-fought independence referendum in 1995 was becoming intense: manufacturing industry was closing, the economy was restructuring and the ubiquitous economic centralisation was bypassing peripheral areas everywhere, and all these issues were taking their toll.

But Quebec has taken a rather different turning from other places, adopting a set of ideas the French call *economie solidaire*, to create the lending institutions that can build up a co-operative network of small businesses; encourage small-scale enterprise and use some of the lessons of development economics, rather than traditional economic policy. The watershed was a summit meeting of the different sectors held in 1996, which led to the creation of a series of institutions designed to provide the finance in hard-to-reach neighbourhoods, and a collection of co-op networks known as the *Chantier de l'economie sociale*, which has driven the development of co-operative enterprise ever since.

Quebec's trade unions had laid the foundations for this success 15 years before when they decided to take a more pro-active stance, setting up a series of revolving investment funds to develop the co-operative enterprise sector.

"The barriers erected by financial institutions became the incentive to design alternatives that would not meet the resistance of mainstream finance," wrote Professor Marguerite Mendell at Concordia University.[6] "Moreover, it was necessary to replicate the lending and investment opportunities available to the private sector, to dispel the myth that social economy enterprises are not investment worthy."

This bold shift in approach delivered results: within five years Quebec's 'social economy' included over 7,800 enterprises.[7] Part of what made Quebec's ultra-local economics policies successful was the concentration on two kinds of co-ops in particular: small-scale care co-ops which could provide sustainable jobs and low-cost social care, and childcare co-ops (nearly a thousand of those had been launched by 2002) to provide low cost nursery schooling. By 2008, the social care co-ops employed over 8,000 people, and the childcare co-ops over 40,000 people.

The Quebec ultra-local policy has also had an impact on the way public services are delivered, with much more delivery happening through small-scale organisations, many of them co-operatives. It is still the kind of solution which feels more akin to development economics than national economic policy, but it seems to have worked – and it borrowed from the approach taken in the 1980s in the Emilia-Romagna region of Italy, based on an approach to mutual guarantee societies to raise the necessary finance which has not been taken in the UK.

KfW

Another vital institution in this area is the large German development bank KfW. Set up in 1948 under the Marshall Plan KfW has more recently provided the model for the new British Business Bank. Like its UK equivalent, KfW is not a direct lender, but provides capital direct to local co-operative banks and municipal savings banks for investment locally. These banks in turn make loans at 2.65 per cent to homeowners and small businesses to create jobs and to reduce energy waste and carbon.[8]

The German programme now operates on a national scale and invests €1bn a year. It has created and is supporting 368,000 construction jobs, upgrading the housing and commercial sectors. Its commitments come to around €10bn a year and KfW manages to leverage an additional €17bn annually in energy efficiency investment, new build and retrofits to Germany's housing stock. Since 2001 more than 2.5 million homes have been upgraded to high-energy savings standards.

The difference between Germany and the UK is that KfW's low interest loans were allowed by the EU single market state aid rules because they already existed, whereas new schemes to subsidise loans may need permission from the European Commission if they are not set at market rates. That is the conventional explanation, and it might obstruct the UK from providing wholesale loans to Community Development Finance Institutions (CDFIs) at zero per cent, as they do in the USA. In the UK the central bank and Treasury can provide loan bundles to large commercial banks under the Funding for Lending scheme at interest rates of less than one per cent but have not made these available to other financial institutions with clout in local markets.

Banco Palmas

The final example of ultra-local economic policy innovation comes from Brazil. Founded in 1998, Banco Palmas is a community bank covering a series of excluded neighbourhoods on the outskirts of Fortaleza, capital of Ceará, the most impoverished of the Brazilian states. It is a difficult place to live and work: the fifth most unequal city in the world and the thirteenth most dangerous. About 5,000 people a year use the bank's services and its main services are two kinds of local loans:

- Investment loans in *reais* for productive purposes and to help people start businesses or improve their income.
- Consumption loans in a local complementary currency, *palmas*, pegged to the *real*, which are designed for spending – rather than accumulating – within the local economy, where they are accepted.

These techniques are a long way from mainstream, certainly from a UK perspective, but they are happening on a big scale. Banco Palmas has spawned 103 other community banks around Brazil using the same model. Designed as a local consumption currency, *palmas* can only be spent within the area and loans usually range from a value of between 20 to 150 euros, for food, clothing or medicine. Described originally as 'emergency loans', purchases in *palmas* are also given discounts by local businesses. And some people working for local businesses are paid partly in *reais* and partly in *palmas*.

The central bank was initially suspicious of these activities, and particularly of the complementary currency, taking Banco Palmas to court twice, losing on both occasions. This crisis for the central bank brought about a major change of heart and, in 2010, they became active supporters and funders of the community banking movement. Banco Palmas remains in legal limbo, but it now has the wholehearted support of the Government. It is also largely self-funding.[9]

What might this mean in the UK?

Local banks, a national enterprise bank and co-operative public service micro-enterprises are not unknown in the UK. But the given examples either support or depend on local financial institutions which know and understand the local market. In the UK we lack these services, partly for the reasons set out above – and partly because of historic legacies to do with the way banks have been regulated in the UK – but also because we have lost our own tradition of economic innovation at local level. The practical expertise that existed at local level was dispersed when the regional development agencies were abolished in 2010.

Yet, even in the UK, there is an ultra-local economics sector emerging. It is diverse and small-scale, and does not see or describe itself in those terms, but it is there. It emerges from the bundle of ideas around regeneration that is given any of the following labels: asset-based economics, sustainable local economics, community-based economics, resilient local economics, using local resources to develop 'diversity, flexibility and increasing capacity'. There is also considerable literature which sets out evidence of how and why it works.[10]

This emerging *ultra-local* economics sector is about repatriating some economic activity, shortening supply chains, reducing carbon footprints and allowing the local economy to service some of its own demand more – and, by doing so, to soak up the spare capacity in struggling areas. And it is also already remarkably clear about what it believes, broadly that there are assets in communities: knowledge, skills, unused resources, land and buildings and money flows that can be harnessed to support local economic development.

Taking ignored assets and turning them into prosperity is the driver in a sector which already covers community energy, community banking, local procurement and money flows and which already promotes an asset-based understanding that local people are an economic resource, however poor they are.

This ultra-micro approach is based on the following principles that, even in the most distressed areas:

- There is money in *all* communities, but not nearly enough institutions invest locally and those which do exist are often too risk averse to grow local markets.
- There are assets in *all* communities – knowledge, skills, resources, land and buildings – that might be harnessed to support local economic development, despite the lack of skills and capital.
- There is money flowing through *all* local economies but, when there are few local enterprises and supply chains, it tends to flow straight out again.
- There is a sense of place at local level, where many of the economic levers belong.

The question at the heart of *People Powered Prosperity* is whether this ultra-micro, people-powered prosperity approach might form the basis of a practical way forward for places which have been bypassed by the global economy and – if it is – why is it happening so rarely, and why do mainstream economic policy-makers discount it or ignore this kind of ambition?

There are some obvious answers. Perhaps they don't believe it works. Maybe they don't believe it is cost-effective or perhaps they believe that – by ignoring some of the key rules of economics – it may make the situation worse or simply that they fear it is too risky a strategy to pursue. Perhaps they are so deeply steeped in the attitudes of the centre that they find it hard to accept that financial institutions are so ineffective elsewhere. Through our interviews in this project, we have tried to pinpoint precisely what has been getting in the way. These are some of the key intellectual obstacles.

A misunderstanding about the word 'local'

There is an understandable scepticism about precisely what the word 'local' means, especially in policy circles. Does it mean local authorities or regions, or more local still? If it means neighbourhoods, then where are the boundaries? Is it meaningful to talk about local economies at all, given that money and people seep in and out, and the smaller the boundaries, the greater the flux?

On the other hand, there is a sense that some economies use more of their own resources than others. Robert

Mundell's work on Optimal Currency Zones implies there is an area which works more effectively for a currency, though those zones are much bigger than anything we would call 'local'.[11] There are also times when we need to distinguish between the Liverpool and the Manchester economy, for example. Or even the Toxteth economy. Not doing so means that the links – and failures to link – are obscured from view. Nor are the potential solutions.

But there is a more fundamental problem here about the word 'local'. Economic policy-makers regard the term as suspect because it implies something absolute. Worse, it implies protectionism. When local economies can only use *local* suppliers or *local* labour, mainstream economics suggests that costs may rise and the job may not be done as well. If that was to happen across a national economy, procurement costs would undoubtedly go up. Any attempt to limit contracts or employment within boundaries will increase prices and make unemployment worse: there will be tit-for-tat retaliation, ergo one city against another. It may trap people in the poorest places even more than before.

Of course, the extreme opposite approach may end up in the same place. A failure to police monopolies, and a burgeoning size of procurement contracts, may mean that only a handful of suppliers are available for public contracts in their sector. Monopoly, like protectionism, will inexorably raise prices and lower quality. Even so, anyone putting forward an ultra-local approach to enable people-powered prosperity needs to be clear that protectionism is not part of the plan: it is about using wasted resources more effectively

– about tackling specific areas of market failure – and this needs to be happen without putting up barriers to trade.

The equivalent American term is 'self-reliance', which has a political caché among conservatives, but otherwise carries the same problems. The clue to cutting this particular translation knot came from the American economist, attorney and author, Michael Shuman:

> "Self-reliance is not isolation. It is diversification, and it is through diversification that we are building wealth."[12]

It may be, in that case, that the word 'local' is hopelessly obfuscatory. The essence of the people-powered prosperity approach is not barriers, it is the development of enterprise at a much more granular level. It is also a response to evidence from the USA that more economic diversity in a place is correlated with a higher density of locally-owned business. This is therefore not an ultra-local approach, strictly speaking; nor is it really an ultra-small one – it is just as much about local ownership and geographical proximity. It isn't about borders; nor is it just about size. It is about the most effective structure for local economies to underpin prosperity – and that means diverse and, as far as possible, locally owned.

The ultra-local approach is a response to the mainstream emphasis on large business, which appears not to be effective where it is most needed, especially given the research in the USA which shows that locally-owned businesses spends more money locally than those which are owned by absentees – which matters in less advantaged areas.[13]

Also relevant here is the word 'decentralising', because this is an approach which attempts to give cities and towns levers which can be effective for their own economic destinies. It implies no borders, but it does suggest that there may be other levels where it might be possible to intervene effectively.

A confusion about how places develop

Modern orthodoxy suggests that places develop themselves by specialisation, by becoming unique in the marketplace. This is undoubtedly true, but it may not be the whole story.

There are two particular problems with this idea when it comes to adapting it as a means by which cities can drag themselves back into the game. The first is that, in a global marketplace – where anywhere can source anything from anywhere – the opportunities for specialising are severely limited. A handful of cities in the world are going to be able to specialise in electronic goods, or media, or anything else. The days when a town or city would only be competing with others in its own region for the same markets, perhaps a few hundred miles away, have long since disappeared.

The other issue emerges from Jane Jacobs' controversial work on the history of cities.[14] She argues that they have always developed economically, not by specialising, but precisely the reverse – by replacing imports with homegrown versions. Work on regional specialisation in the USA also suggests that it has been in decline since the end of the Second World War.[15] If Jacobs was right, then that must have implications for our understanding of regeneration now. It suggests that what holds cities back isn't so much marketing skills, it is technical ones. What gets in the way isn't so much the failure to attract outside investment, it is the failure to use what skills they already possess. What gets in the way isn't just lack of *external* investment, it is lack of *internal* investment.

Jacobs argued, paradoxically, that local diversification led to more clusters which could specialise and export – and with more security than a city which had one specialisation (like Detroit) and which would suffer if that one specialisation faced a global economic downturn.

Jane Jacobs occupies a peculiar position on the political pantheon, the darling of the development left and of the free market right. She has been hailed by the advocates of the Austrian school of economics for her "innate grasp of the power of voluntary exchange and spontaneous order".[16] Supporters from the right argue that, as such, heavy-handed central planning fails to take account of the subtleties of the knowledge possessed only by the individuals on the scene (for which she coined the term 'locality knowledge'). Her work also implies the critical importance of places being self-aware, and the need for feedback loops – which is why she argues that currencies naturally suit city regions rather than nations.[17]

None of this suggests that everything can be produced locally, and no specialisation should be permitted, though that is often the fear in the mainstream. Who could deal with every village making their own smartphones, after all? The point is whether, to mop up spare capacity in some places, there may be scope for *more* local production

– especially as fuel prices are likely to raise the cost of transport eventually (notwithstanding recent price falls). If that can be done without putting up trade barriers, without raising costs or undermining quality – so that local producers can compete on more equal terms – then that fulfils Jane Jacobs' vision: diversity and choice.

The original thinking behind Michael Heseltine's City Challenge scheme recognised some of this: the sheer complexity of cities and neighbourhoods could only be understood locally. That is also the thinking behind City Deals in recent years, but the underlying logic – that cities have hidden, wasted resources that can only be accessed locally – has fed into the development of local skills, but not yet beyond that.

Michael Shuman (see page 24) argues that local development requires all the elements to work together – local planning (ambiguous, at best, under the UK National Planning Framework), local purchasing (allowed under the Social Value Act but not encouraged), local people (lack of local institutions in the UK), local investing (ditto in the UK), local partnerships (beginning between local businesses in the UK, but slowly) and local public policy (which is where the debate currently stands). These elements have not yet been gathered together as one idea here, though the new devolution of power to Manchester and other cities may lead to that.

The fear of displacement and deadweight

The Enterprise Allowance Scheme was introduced in 1983 and was considered to be hugely successful at the time. But the evaluations told a rather different story. All similar schemes to encourage self-employment suffer from high levels of 'displacement' and 'deadweight'.[18] All too often they move service work around the area – minicabs or hairdressing – either bankrupting themselves or another similar business. One in six recipients were unemployed again within a year, and those that did succeed rarely employed anyone else.[19] If they did succeed, we can never really know whether they would have succeeded anyway and the resources put into the scheme were therefore a 'deadweight' loss to society.

This clearly is a problem if the population is steady and the only enterprises are servicing a limited pool of local people. There is a limited number of times a set population will need to get its hair cut, after all. If there are unused resources, and unmet needs, there will need to be other ways to connect these without simply shifting demand from one place to another.

But the fear of displacement has led mainstream policy-makers to assume too easily that this will always be the case where areas are struggling. Because there certainly are counter examples, either because the new enterprises attract people and customers from outside, or because they replace outside services which take spending power away from local people. Both of these can potentially deal with the market failure that undermines impoverished economies. Even displacement business will improve local services, if people use it, and expanding the number and range of locally-owned businesses has an important economic and social role. In practice, most sectors in poorer areas are importing services from wealthier areas, which is part of their basic problem.[20]

The issue with the idea that displacement will always undermine new self-employment is that it assumes that no variation in the size of the economy is possible – the Lump of Labour Fallacy[21] in reverse (the evidence is that Uber grows the taxi market, for example, rather than simply displacing existing taxis).[22]

But this fundamental assumption was challenged by Jim O'Neill's recent report for the City Growth Commission.[23] The traditional Treasury model seems to imply that there is no 'additionality' – that any success in one place has to happen as a result of moving that success from somewhere else. That any prosperity in the regions has to be an opportunity cost, and an opportunity lost, in London.

This is, of course, something of a caricature, and the Treasury have now accepted some of O'Neill's argument that there are opportunities being lost in the cities, and that – if they can reach the success of London – there is a potential £79bn to be added to the national growth figures by 2030.[24] On the other hand, the Treasury is clearly right to insist on minimising the deadweight effect of badly designed interventions, and to remain sceptical of some claims for additionality, given that they are sceptical also about how this local growth might be achieved. In the end, the ultra-local argument comes down to the same, very pragmatic conundrum: will it work?

**

These are three reasons why there has been difficulty in this discussion – the ambiguities about 'local' action, especially if it leads to protectionism, the unresolved debate about how cities develop their economies in the first place, and the argument about whether you can grow local economies at all.

All these are reasonable objections, but the market failure of disadvantaged cities and neighbourhood remains. The next chapter sets out three reasons why a different approach is justified – involving some rethinking about:

- How success is measured.
- How better local information is required.
- How local market failure demands exceptions to some of the usual rules.

4. Towards people-powered prosperity

We suggest three ways forward to bring the two sides – mainstream and radical – together for the benefit of cities and towns:

- Success needs to be measured in ways more in line with the Treasury Green Book and some way beyond Gross Value Added (GVA).
- Institutions capable of nurturing small enterprises need access to very local information which national institutions find it nigh on impossible to seek out.
- Local market failure requires measures that can privilege small enterprise to provide more choice in certain disadvantaged areas.

It is clear so far that misunderstandings about local approaches to economic redevelopment may be holding back innovation. It is also clear that part of these approaches involve fallacies which the mainstream tells itself, and which involve particular confusions at local level.

These fallacies include, for example, the idea that poor people must not be trapped in failing areas when we know that many of them will not in fact move. Another, set out below, is the fallacy involving the measurement of economic success. The Treasury *Green Book* is an exemplar of good, pragmatic sense – the difficulty is that, in practice, most arms of government, central and local, use a different approach to measurement entirely.

The great measurement muddle

Most governments, including our own, measure the success of their economic policies region by region, as they should do. They measure it using a measure known as Gross Value Added or GVA. This is a measure of the real value of goods and services produced in any given area, excluding intermediate consumption – in other words, that part of the output used in the production of other outputs.

Measuring Regional GVA is a legal requirement of the European Union. There is no choice about whether it is done or how it is done. It is calculated across the EU at different levels for each nation, broadly down to county level, known in the trade by the jargon NUTS (Nomenclature of Units for Territorial Statistics).

But there are obvious drawbacks to measuring success this way alone. Like Gross Domestic Product (GDP), GVA simply measures the level of economic activity in a given nation, region or sector. While this is useful, it doesn't adequately reflect the important things that we need to know. Problems with GVA include:

- It does not tell us about the distribution of economic activity, whether this is concentrated among a few narrow groups or whether it is spread evenly.
- It is not always clear what is actual value added output and what is simply dealing with the costs of other economic activity. For example, environmental improvements may represent a genuine addition to value, or they could be just addressing the side effects of production elsewhere.
- It doesn't factor in things like the costs of having to support failing neighbourhoods with welfare.

A reliance on GVA by itself assumes that, if you invest in the best return, then the rewards will trickle down to the other places – it assumes that there are no asymmetries, that all the information is perfect, and that competition is on a level playing field. In fact, since none of these things are true, GVA by itself is simply a measure of market power – the GVA of the financial sector is arguably as much about its ability to charge too much as it is about its real success.

Using GDP as the single measure of success can blind policy-makers to the imbalance in the rewards. It can result in one-sided policies which benefit a few people or places rather than the rest. In the same way, GVA as a single measure can benefit some sectors, cities or communities at the expense of others. In short, it can still leave some neighbourhoods and cities struggling, despite the local resources which lie idle: people, buildings and raw materials. Using GVA alone, or putting too much emphasis on GVA in decision-making, can intensify the basic problem which *People Powered Prosperity* is attempting to tackle: where some places get sidelined by success.

Using GVA as your only measure might involve building a marina, and a few luxury businesses to serve it, and congratulating yourself that the local GVA is rising, though it might have involved no change to the previous economy.

There is evidence that GVA needs to be balanced by employment growth (though clearly this also needs to be balanced by some kind of measure of local income and prosperity). Between 2001 and 2008, cities with the highest increases in employment, not GVA, were most successful in reducing poverty.[25] Output growth had no short-term impact on urban poverty. It is associated with wage increases at the top of the distribution but not wages at the bottom. In the long term, output growth may lead to employment growth and this may then reduce poverty, but in the long run – as Keynes famously put it – we are all dead.[26]

The problem with GVA is not that it isn't useful – it clearly is – but, if it is the only measure used, then it will distort the way in which policy-makers regard the problem. The GVA of a city will look broadly at the money earned, taking no account of how that income was distributed, how the earnings were distributed – whether it was a handful of sectors earning it all while other sectors struggled independently. It takes no account of the purchasing power of those earnings, the value of money in different sectors and different places. Above all, it takes no account of economic efficiency – whether the GVA arose from the genuine creation of new wealth, or by extracting wealth from elsewhere through exercising monopoly market power.[27]

The Green Book

Despite the widespread use of GVA as a decision-making tool, the Treasury's evaluation bible, known as the 'Green Book', never mentions GVA. The latest version of *The Green Book* is updated all the time, but dates back to 2003. It is an enlightened and balanced guide to the pros and cons of different kinds of analysis.

The Green Book couldn't be clearer that the distribution of benefits has to be taken into account in decision-making:

> "It is important that the distributional implications of each option are considered during appraisal. This type of analysis enhances the understanding of the fairness of proposals, their social impacts and their scale. The impact of a policy, programme or project on an individual's well-being will vary according to his or her income; the rationale being that an extra pound will give more benefit to a person who is deprived than to someone who is well off. In economics, this concept is known as the 'diminishing marginal utility of additional consumption'."[28]

It goes on to explain that proposals might have different impacts on different sectors, and that "these effects should be explicitly stated and quantified wherever feasible".

But there is nonetheless an element of bias in *The Green*

Book for what The Treasury call the 'maximin-return' option, which they describe as "the most important to consider", on the grounds that it "provides the least bad outcome if the worst possible conditions prevail". The 'maximin-return option' is not necessarily the one designated by an analysis of GVA, but because GVA is the simplest measure, and maximising GVA seems like the simplest option from London, that may mean that GVA becomes a default measure in Whitehall, just as it does in the regions.

That explains the emphasis on GVA for the Local Enterprise Partnerships, and the laborious business of calculating GVA on LEP boundaries back to 1997.[29] The overwhelming use of GVA is apparent, for example, if you glance at the development of the new London Economic Development Plan. The plan, due in early 2015, is being developed by the business lobby group London First and the consultants McKinsey, who have been using what they call a "data driven approach" using GVA. They describe this as:

> "Prioritising London's resources so as to focus on the areas which, objectively, offer the best return."[30]

This is what GVA does. It provides an indication of the best returns for investment, and where to prioritise resources for the best financial return on capital. But we also need to be clear what it fails to do: it doesn't provide any indication of the best way of using wasted economic resources at local level. It doesn't indicate how to reduce the welfare dependency of some areas. It doesn't indicate how the success might be distributed differently.

The question is not whether GVA is the *right* measure to use – it may be or it may not, depending on how it is used – but whether any measure can possibly be useful if it is the *only* one.

Other measures

We have already suggested that the in-built bias towards GVA as the single measure to evaluate policy at regional level – though this is not supported explicitly in *The Green Book* at the Treasury – may unnecessarily blind policy-makers to the potential of using wasted economic resources more effectively. This does not rule out GVA, but it suggests it needs to be used alongside a basket of other measures. One of these will clearly be job creation, but even that can be misleading on its own. The new report on strategic transport by consultants Volterra Partners suggest a mixed approach along these lines, which would refine the GVA benefits of potential projects with their impact on welfare payments not paid and reductions in carbon.[31]

The Community Development Finance Association and their backers at Citibank commissioned an alternative basket of measures for evaluating their own economic impact.[32] Among the measures they recommended were:

- Increased entrepreneurship.
- Growth in business stock.
- Growth in employment.
- Resilience and diversity in the local economy.

They also proposed a series of social measures like poverty, well-being and carbon emissions, but it is the other economic measures that concern us here. The authors were searching for a way of measuring impact that looks not just at the direct impacts, but also at the wider changes that beneficiaries from loans create in their own ec onomic and social systems. How much, for example, an investment will lead to spending by their suppliers and their employees which increase the multiplier, nationally and – crucially if we are trying to tackle wasted economic assets – locally as well.

Equally, of course, the same beneficiary might take business away from an existing local company: this is the phenomenon of 'displacement' we discussed earlier. On the other hand, it might allow an individual to pay off a short-term loan at high interest, saving interest payments to distant loan companies, and put the money in a savings scheme which stops them being cut off by their gas supplier. It saves worry and stress, and it also saves the cost of disconnection. Any useful evaluation scheme needs to make these kinds of distinctions, and to work out how much the wider impact falls inside the local boundaries and how much outside.

These distinctions are difficult to estimate but this does not make them pointless.

Resilience, personal and economic, is also a difficult area, because it seems to run counter to population churn. It has the same kind of contradictions as measuring well-being because it runs counter to one of the prime accepted objectives of regeneration: to allow the population to leave a failing area. Measures of resilience will often mean people are enabled to stay put. The danger is that accepted measures may rule out resilience because it seems to be trapping people in poor areas, whereas it is actually saving public money by reducing social churn.

Other areas where we need data include the percentage of local jobs in locally-owned businesses, the annual reduction in economic leakage from the area, the survival rate of start-ups, the percentage of business in an area measuring triple-bottom line performance.

Reasons for action

The Green Book is clear about the reasons why governments act:

> "This underlying rationale is usually founded either in market failure or where there are clear government distributional objectives that need to be met. Market failure refers to where the market has not and cannot of itself be expected to deliver an efficient outcome..."[33]

People Powered Prosperity argues that mainstream economic policy-making needs to look for more local economic tools if it is going to tackle market failure at local level. The difficulty is that conventional thinking, buttressed by an over-reliance on estimates of GVA, tends to focus on measures that can maximise a national return, rather than looking for local measures that might – at lower cost – allow some areas to use the economic resources available to them more effectively.

There will always be a more lucrative place to invest tax revenue that would achieve better growth than investing in poorer places. That is the danger of too much reliance on GVA.

This is what one of our interviewees called 'The Lazy Treasury Get-Out'. It suggests that the Government should tax people in order to invest this money only where it can expect a better market return. This has a series of unattractive, and largely undiscussed, side-effects:

- It means that ordinary people on low and moderate income will have to hand over their money to the Government, but only the areas with the most market potential will benefit from the investment of that same tax revenue – which may often be wealthier ones.
- It also means the rich win twice: they can afford the taxes *and* they get the benefits of the investment too.
- It also threatens to crowd out genuine business investment, because the Government is doing it instead.

That is the danger of single measures of success, and GVA in particular. It tends to limit government investment to places that can earn better market returns, and is unfair on those who pay taxes, only to have them spent on the places that are already brimming with potential. It undermines the chances of investment, or building institutions, with the purpose of allowing less successful areas to tackle the inefficiency of their economies. It risks condemning the less successful places to a life everlastingly dependent on welfare, simply because the objectives of reducing welfare dependency will never measure up to the kind of market returns possible elsewhere.

Ironically, it need not do so, and the *Green Book* sets out how to avoid it. The problem is that GVA tends not to be operated along those lines in practice.

Big data

There used to be a reason why local economic levers were ignored. The vast majority of the basic information flowing into the Treasury was national data. The currency was managed nationally. The levers were national ones. Of course it made sense for all economic policy to be managed nationally. What has changed is the advent of 'big data'.

It is a phrase on everyone's lips these days. Whether or not it is going to change the world in quite the way its enthusiasts predict remains to be seen, but it is certainly important. Companies like Walmart keep data on a million customer transactions every hour. The volume of business data available is now doubling every 14 months. There is data available about energy use, public health, driving times, weather and a whole range of other behaviour, social and natural. And it is used: data miners dice it this way and that, supercomputers analyse it, allowing managers, doctors and analysts to intervene early, to sort out blockages and leaks, to save energy and make the world turn a little more efficiently.

Big data means that we can sub-divide bank lending down to ward level, obesity and diabetes down to street level. We can watch the development of whole cities street by street, using online techniques and call centres as they do in New York City or San Francisco.[34]

By getting a bird's eye view of any given situation, it means we can clear logjams, tackle difficulties and focus resources. We can make systems work better. But there is one area of modern life which is apparently immune from the revolution in big data: mainstream economic policy is nervous about tackling economic logjams at local level. We can watch the flow of energy around local systems, or the flow of traffic around a city, but we seem to have no interest in watching the flow of money around a city.

It isn't that we have no information. The data on bank lending, mortgages and personal loans, postcode by postcode, was extracted from the big banks by members of the House of Lords in 2013. We know a great deal about the so-called super output areas. Local authorities have labour statistics, claimant figures. Their difficulties are twofold:

- Towns and cities have very little information about local money flows, skill needs, investments and trends.
- Mainstream economic policy has tended to shun this kind of detail.

The real difference is not that the data could never be available – it is that, for reasons now lost to public debate, we don't think it is worth using the data locally. We don't believe it is important enough.

When Keynes urged that, "above all, let finance be national", he was defying people who wanted it to be international.[35] But although mainstream economic policy-making has now largely rejected the Keynesian legacy, they cling to his idea – taken out of context – that the basic economic unit is national. Growth figures, employment figures and money supply figures are all national. They can be aggregated together to make international data, and are occasionally disaggregated down to city or regional level. But the idea that we might *use* big data to get a bird's eye view of economies on any more local basis than that appears to be anathema to economic policy-makers.

Big data is potentially revolutionising application in medicine, local administration, welfare and astronomy. It makes a forensic focus on precise spots of constipation possible. So why not in economics? Big data allows us to look at the body like a detailed map, so why not the body economic? Why not look in forensic detail where the money goes? It is true that local resources are also national resources – but not true the other way around, and the levers for accessing those local resources may be primarily at local level. The question is whether by failing to look more closely, and because of the measuring tools we use, we miss the ways in which money flows get stuck – or just flow in and straight out again. Perhaps by failing to track those money flows in detail around disadvantaged areas, we are missing a more precise opportunity to make our own economies work more effectively.

The tools for doing so are in their earliest stages.[36] But it makes no sense for cities or towns to miss out on the revolution being offered by big data analysis.

The search for information

It is increasingly clear that there is a problem with the way that mainstream economic development supports new businesses, even successful ones, if they are smaller. National banking infrastructure finds this demonstrably difficult, especially in the UK where the total volume of credit to SMEs has only just begun to recover since the disasters of 2008.

The precise data in the UK about the contribution made by smaller businesses is not as well researched as it is in the USA, but we have to assume there are parallels. In 2010, *Harvard Business Review* published a graph along with the headline 'More small firms means more jobs'.[37] The article said:

> "Our research shows that regional economic growth is highly correlated with the presence of many small, entrepreneurial employers—not a few big ones."

Authors argued that the arrival of a big company in a local or regional economy might have little comparative effect on employment, "even when they are doing well". There was more support for this position from *Economic Development Quarterly* which found that:

> "Economic growth models that control for other relevant factors reveal a positive relationship between density of

locally owned firms and per capita income growth, but only for small (10-99 employees) firms, whereas the density of large (more than 500 workers) firms not owned locally has a negative effect."[38]

The implication is not just that SMEs are vital for local economies, especially when they are owned and managed nearby, but also for the national economy. The question then is what has traditionally prevented UK financial institutions investing in SMEs, or providing them with adequate credit support as they expand? Mainstream policy-makers tend to take their cues from the big banks and assume that the absence of lending to local SMEs, and indeed the absence of local financial institutions in an area, are both a sign of lack of demand. The evidence for this is highly contested; it looks more like a major market failure.

Sunspots and co-ordination

Many local economies find themselves caught in a vicious cycle. Failing local businesses create deprived areas of boarded up shops and run-down residential areas. Faced with this poor environment, essential resources escape the area. People who are better educated move away and money is invested elsewhere. Starved of these resources, local businesses struggle even more and the cycle continues.

Of course, the cycle can also go the other way. A blossoming local economy can lead to urban improvements that turn a once run-down area into one that is seen as up-and-coming. Skills move into the area as more mobile people actively choose to live there. Money flows in as investment prospects are seen to improve. This gives a further boost to local business and the virtuous cycle continues.

But what decides whether a local economy is in a vicious cycle or a virtuous one? Sometimes, it can be no more than a self-fulfilling belief. Each pattern of events represents a valid equilibrium result and the economy in question just happens to have fallen into one rather than the other. If people believe that things will develop a particular way, then they act accordingly and sometimes this is enough to make sure those expectations are realised, good or bad. Once a local economy is in a bad equilibrium, it may at some stage switch to a good one, but there is no guarantee.

This type of equilibrium, where one possible outcome is sustained simply by people's expectations, is known as a sunspot.[39] With sunspot equilibriums, no economy can be relied upon to shift from a bad outcome to a good one without some kind of an outside stimulus. On the other hand, once a shift has been achieved, the economy should stay in that good equilibrium of its own accord.

Given the way sunspots work, then tackling the decline of local economies may be, to a large extent, a question of co-ordination. If enough combined impetus can be organised, it may be sufficient to shift the local economy off the bad path and onto the good path. Although this may still require some form of initial investment, the benefits of moving to the better equilibrium should easily repay this.

The best example of this is in the value of property. Shifting the belief of property investors from outside the area is enough to transform the bricks and mortar of a place.

It is an approach that dates back to the development corporations of the Heseltine era and of Margaret Thatcher's Action for Cities (1987). It works, if your ambitions are confined to the physical fabric of a place, but it can also raise property prices so that it becomes unaffordable for the people who were born and bred there. Their problem isn't solved – nor is the problem of scaling up these successes to a wider area. It might work for the Isle of Dogs or Salford Quays, but it isn't enough for Bradford or Barrow. It isn't so much economic development as town and country planning.

But imagine that local institutions existed which allowed local people to co-ordinate their resources to achieve a better economic future for themselves – attracting the kind of entrepreneurs, or the right small investments, that can revitalise the economy in ways that take people with them. In the medium-term, this may also increase property prices and drive out the local people – London suburbs like Crystal Palace seem to be on the verge of this – but they might do so slowly and interestingly enough to make a permanent difference, and do so in an inclusive way. The so-called sharing economy, which provides the infrastructure – usually online – which allows people to share or profit from their assets, from spare rooms to car park spaces – is an example of co-ordination, and especially perhaps the examples which are mutually owned (like Wikipedia and Couchsurfing). It is already happening and appears to now be worth approximately £500m to the UK economy, and is predicted to rise to £9bn by 2025.[40] Some of this is clearly money being moved from the formal to less formal economy, but some of Airbnb's clients are undoubtedly earning more money – certainly for the neighbourhood and probably for the nation as a whole. Co-ordination isn't necessarily a zero-sum game. But it does make local information a critical factor in any kind of local development.

Information and externalities

Information plays an important role in economic analysis. Optimal outcomes often depend on the existence of perfect information. In reality, information is limited and can be expensive. We have to make choices between incurring costs to improve information or risking sub-optimal outcomes. We know, for example, that the main constraint on lending to poorer people is the cost of gathering information about them.[41]

This is a key area of disagreement between the advocates of ultra-local and mainstream policy-makers, but it is an important one, because one advantage of very local institutions is that they have higher levels of community knowledge. In the Brazilian community banks (see page 18), credit officers don't collect electronic or even written information, but walk into the community and chat not only with the applicant but also with her neighbours. The costs of finding that extra local information are also usually lower for a locally rooted institution. In general, the more granular the approach, the better the quality of the information is likely to be. An individual or household is well placed to value the different potential outcomes to which it might be subject, including those elements which cannot be accurately valued by revealed preference. The more we move away from the individual unit, the harder it becomes to value such things.

One reason local investors in the USA seem to have such a record of success is that they visit the company they are investing in, become advocates, supporters and advisors to it in a way a large banking organisation can never do.[42]

This information gradient is particularly important when it comes to externalities. Due to their very nature, the market provides no guidance about the value of externalities. If we want to factor them in, we have to stay to make an informed assessment. Information is key and there is more than one kind of information – there is data, but there is also the kind of informal information that is much better assessed face to face, in a way that the bigger banks and lenders that rely on centralised credit scoring systems are unable to do.

Local initiatives tend to pay more attention to the value of externalities – the social and environmental costs and benefits. For example the Community Energy Strategy from the Department of Energy and Climate Change noted "a focus on social outcomes, rather than only financial benefit for shareholders" as an important feature of community energy projects.[43] The Environmental Protection Agency in the USA has found that emissions are lower for industrial plants that are owned locally. These findings should come as no surprise. At the local and community level, there is a much greater awareness of the value of these factors. It is therefore easier to incorporate them into the decision making process.

Information and finance

Information also plays an important role in the provision of finance. The contractual relationship between lender and borrower inevitably involves some element of asymmetric information. Borrowers have better knowledge of their prospects and of their actual outcomes. Lenders face a pay-off between the level of uncertainty they accept and the level of costs they incur to improve their information. Either way, the return they demand is higher, and the quantity of funding provided is probably also lower, than would hold with perfect information. This excess return or reduced funding represents a deadweight loss to the economy. It is a critical missing element in mainstream policy-maker's understanding of how local economies work.

As economists, policy-makers are of course aware of the theoretical difficulties, but as civil servants in central government, they have become too reliant on central data. They put too much weight on it; they are blind to its defects and omissions, rather as the big banks are. But the big banks are more aware of the missing information, which is why local lending is so difficult for them, since they have no 'boots on the ground'.

The greater the extent of public information, therefore, the less the deadweight loss. A key element of local finance initiatives is that they rely on the higher level of community knowledge. Being more directly involved in the local community, lenders have naturally better access to information about local business. Even when finance is provided from outside the area, local organisations can reduce the information deadweight loss. Mutual guarantee arrangements can take advantage of relationships that exist at the local level to improve the risk for outside investors.[44]

The implications

The argument for focus on local enterprise is as follows: there is a relationship between diverse, inter-connected and locally-owned businesses and local prosperity, assuming US research applies also to the UK (see page 49). The main barrier to nurturing local enterprise is that national banking infrastructure, using risk evaluation software from regional offices, is compromised – because it lacks the information required to take effective decisions. This suggests that we need more financial institutions which deliberately limit their sphere of influence to the city or region, like Sparkassen in Germany and nearly all the credit unions (VanCity, for example) in North America.

This is true, but there is an important counter-argument which highlights the complexity involved. It makes sense that local enterprise might have access to the savings of neighbours, which would otherwise be invested by the big banks (which have a necessarily myopic understanding of local opportunities), but there are risks if those are the only funds available to them – because it would make them doubly vulnerable to a city or regional crisis or downturn. There are risks to local interdependence, and too much local inter-connectivity, which any ultra-local policy must take seriously: in practice, the solution is appropriate geographical scale and for very small institutions to

co-operate with others in networks – not too small for
security, not too big to lose local information – perhaps
sometimes West Yorkshire rather than Bradford. But
investing in companies you are close to can still help fill the
information gap and encourage better allocation of capital,
and provide supportive, long-term investors for businesses.[45]
As always, there is a balance to be struck.

Creating local financial institutions which can rely only
on local deposits to fund credit is only going to go so far,
especially in places which are seriously impoverished. That
implies that we also need to look at ways for investment to
flow from wealthy areas to poorer ones, rather than always
the other way round.

We know that SMEs make up more than 99 per cent of
the businesses in the UK, that they employ about half the
working population in the UK, and are at least as profitable as
their larger competitors.[46] In the USA most sectors of the
economy have more examples of very competitive smaller
businesses than large ones, though – like here – the smaller
ones operate under the disadvantage that investment and
supportive banking services are harder to get hold of. This
profitability is important. According to OECD figures, SMEs
in the UK earn just over half (51%) of economic value added
compared to businesses of more than 250 employees.[47] If our
banking systems were working efficiently, at least half of
savings deposits would be used to fund credit to small
businesses. If our capital markets were working efficiently, at
least half of our investment in securities would be reinvested
in small businesses.

That balance is not being achieved, which means that

investment is being wasted on less successful businesses, because the institutions which could run effective SME lending barely exist. This is a market failure of huge proportions, and the lack of local financial institutions is only a part of this much bigger problem.

Because of their lack of useable local information, the financial sector is facilitating the shift of resources from the poor to the rich, from poor areas to rich areas, and from black minority ethnic (BME) communities to white ones. The traditional ultra-local solutions may be inadequate for the task, but either way this is a market failure of monumental proportion that urgently demands solutions.

Tackling local market failure

A commitment to free trade runs deep in the British psyche. It is rooted in history, with political resistance in the nineteenth century against import tariffs on grain imports (the Corn Laws) uniting the new professional middle classes with urban industrial workers against the vested interests of landowners.[48] It is well grounded in economics too, with Ricardo's theory of comparative advantage having stood the test of time as an elegant explanation of how we gain from specialising in what we do best and trading with others.[49] Finally, there is the simple but compelling attraction of the phase: whatever the alternative to 'free' is, it probably doesn't sound preferable.

No wonder that calls for localism in economics set policymakers' teeth on edge. It can sound like little more than an attempt to shelter inefficient or uncompetitive local producers from competition. Although Ricardo was addressing trade between nations, this suspicion of protectionism thwarting efficient use of resources applies to trade between different areas within a nation too.

But it would be wrong to dismiss out of hand any pro-active attempt to foster more localised production. There may still be circumstances, and places, where it remains useful. To understand why, we need to first unpack the conditions under which unfettered markets lead to the most positive societal outcomes by maximising production and, hence, consumption. Economics concerns itself with efficiency, and how best to use the nation's resources – people, capital and natural endowment – to maximise production. Market economies achieve this by distributing decisions about resource allocation to tens of millions of economic actors - customers and suppliers - interacting with one another in open markets. The price mechanism provides the signals and feedback to adjust production and resource use to match ever-changing relative costs of production and consumer demands.

So far, so good, but, as every economist knows, unregulated markets will achieve the best outcomes only under certain conditions, for example where competition and information is good – and often it isn't. In fact, many economic activities exist only because such perfect market conditions don't exist (estate agents and insurance, for example).[50] This is not an argument against markets in general – quite the reverse – but it does recognise that governments need to act when markets fail, as the Treasury's *Green Book* suggests.

So under what specific conditions might markets fail to produce the greatest societal good? There are three that are most pertinent to local economies:

- Social and environmental externalities.
- Distorted market power.
- Unbalanced labour mobility.

We will also consider the concept of economic resilience, which questions whether pursuing economic efficiency in the short-term, at the expense of losing system resilience, might actually undermine success over the longer term.

Social and environmental externalities

If production or consumption causes environmental or social harm that is not recognised by markets, then resources have been misallocated. The concept of 'externalities' – costs that are not reflected (or internalised) in market prices – is universally accepted within economic theory. Where differences arise, it is usually over the extent to which such externalities exist in any particular case.

Take food miles, for example. If carbon emissions from transporting food are not fully reflected in costs, supplies from large scale food service companies will be underpriced relative to local producers. The Bank of England made this point in a recent paper on local currencies, an economic instrument that deliberately disturbs the free flow of goods and services between regions within the UK:

> "If non-local goods are cheaper because market prices do not fully factor in the additional costs that they impose on society over locally produced goods — for instance, higher carbon emissions as a result of increased transportation — then local currencies may improve welfare."[51]

Or take, as an example of social externalities, the benefit to society of favouring suppliers that aim to reskill marginalised workers in areas of deprivation and high unemployment, for example ex-offenders or NEETS (young people not in employment, education or training). Such workers might be expected to be less productive than those in economically successful regions, but the positive externality of improving the productivity of workers in less successful regions can't be captured by local companies in the prices they charge – unless procurement practices allow them to.

Tailoring public policy to avoid these externalities at ultra-local level will involve supporting small scale local enterprises with specific environmental and socially beneficial impacts, and made possible only because they are local small scale enterprises – for example, community energy installations, and other co-ops running amenities like those in Quebec (see page 15). Since 2013, the Social Value Act has required public bodies to consider this issue when they commission services and award contracts. Rather than choosing the lowest cost provider, they can choose a higher cost supplier if it creates a greater social benefit in the area. There may, in certain circumstances, be justifications for privileging small businesses in distinct areas.

Distorted competition

The concept of competition is so familiar and simple in everyday usage that it is easy to lose sight of the complexities and nuances of competition in practice. The pure assumption of free markets is that a large number of firms compete on equal terms. None has any greater market power than the others and firms can easily enter and leave the market. But most industries don't have these characteristics, and for very good reasons.

One is the need for scale. Some goods are more efficiently produced in large volumes and require huge capital investment (think aircraft or superconductors). Similarly, some services only work if they are widely adopted (think Facebook or Google). Economies of scale sometimes require us to have a handful of producers with great market power.

Another reason is that some firms will be more successful than others. A market might start out with a large number of evenly matched competitors but, sooner or later, winners will emerge and losers will leave the market. The winners might grow and accumulate market power leading to the paradox that, over time, free competition tends to erode free competition (think supermarkets versus local independent grocers and food markets).

Such uneven markets might still be competitive if the powerful incumbents at least face constant challenges from dynamic and innovative new players to keep them on their toes. But in many cases, small companies, which by nature are quite local, suffer from a distorted market where they just can't compete on level terms with large national, or international corporates. The advantages that accrue to the latter are not necessarily genuine economic efficiencies. For example, steep discounts from their suppliers obtained by large corporations might reflect excessive market power rather than efficiencies of reduced transaction costs. The main supermarket chains can buy goods from food suppliers at significantly lower prices than independent retailers, but accusations of market abuse suggest this is often the exercise of monopoly power.[52] In such circumstances, polices and tools that aim to 'level the playing field' by favouring small local producers can lead to an overall welfare gain by addressing a market failure.

Ultra-local policies might include reducing the size of procurement contracts so that local businesses can manage them – or other ways that privilege local suppliers, like secondary currency systems or providing local enterprises with very low interest credit. It might also mean looking more closely at the imbalance in financial outcomes. Why for example have banks and investors failed to serve the local investment needs of small business? Should we look again at bank regulations that over-regulate small banks with approaches designed for big banks, or which over-regulate investments in small business along with big ones, and by doing so make them much more difficult?

The failure of local economies may reflect the failure of financial institutions to deal more effectively with their investment needs, dismissing too easily the people who live there, and failing to recognise their needs and potential resources.

Labour mobility and immobility

The final area of market failure concerns the assumption that labour will move to where the jobs are. As we discussed earlier (see page 10), this is not how it plays out when areas start to do badly economically. Labour mobility is uneven in many ways, but often struggling places will lose the middle classes and lose young people. Homeowners and private renters with good employment incomes can move more easily than social tenants. They also tend to have the personal resourcefulness to manage the many changes required, such as transferring schools and medical providers.

People in low paid work, with chronic ill-health, or on benefits will find it much more difficult to move. Young adults, particularly without any family commitments, are also more mobile and may naturally seek the excitement of London or big city life. This adverse selection in labour mobility means that areas that are in economic decline will have fewer of the young, healthy, resourceful, well-off and ambitious – exactly the workers needed to help reverse the decline.

Ultra-local policies to tackle this might include measures to help retain graduates, like Bournemouth's business start-up loans and mortgages for young graduates to keep them in the town, or Northumbria University's enterprise centre.[53] They might involve policies that keep middle class career paths in the regions, rather than forcing them into jobs in London – or investment in systems that allow knowledge workers to work anywhere, like better trains or broadband.

The importance of economic resilience

These market failures usually justify intervention to promote people-powered prosperity in a way that is consistent with, indeed validated by, orthodox neo-classical economic theory. But just as important are the recent developments in systems thinking that have focused on the role of the *resilience* of the economic system as distinct from its *efficiency*.[54]

Resilience describes the capacity of a system to deal successfully with shocks. What 'success' might mean in this context requires further definition, and in a report by the New Economics Foundation prepared for the Friends Provident Foundation, economic resilience was defined with reference to economic, social and environmental outcomes:

> "Economic resilience is the capacity of an economic system to adapt in the face of both short-term shocks and long-term changes in ecological, social and economic conditions with the aim of supporting the community to thrive whilst using its fair share of ecological resources."[55]

This reflects an adaptive or evolutionary understanding of resilience, as opposed to equilibrium approaches, associated with orthodox economics, which focus on a system's ability to return to a steady state following a disturbance. It also emphasises that we must think about system resilience in the context of the system's purpose. For example, following the global financial crisis of 2007-8 the financial system has arguably proved 'resilient' in terms of its ability to return swiftly to 'business as usual' (with the help of enormous government support) but not in terms of its ability to fulfil its social function or to adapt to changing circumstances.

Local systems need the capacity to innovate and learn if they are going to adapt. One way they can do this is by fostering diversity among their economic actors, including actors with a geographical focus and knowledge. This means that the system can respond in the right way to specific local conditions, but it can also innovate – and the innovation can be replicated and scaled elsewhere.

It is not clear whether small or large firms are best at innovating – it is a contested debate in economics.[56] But it is clear that both play a role, so we hardly need to wait for a universal conclusion – and, in any case, it depends on what field of innovation we are talking about. There are some kinds of innovation – often social innovations – that can create social and economic value in specific local circumstances, and which require a sufficient range of small-scale local enterprises.

Resilience thinking and the disciplines it draws on – such as ecological science and complexity theory – are beginning to pose a challenge to mainstream economic policy where it fails to understand the important role of regional and local economies in the national picture, because it tends to emphasise efficiency over resilience. It often fails to see there is a trade-off to be made between the two.

We need to shape more resilient local economies partly because the social and economic costs of economic crashes are so extensive – we need to make sure that policies aimed at maximising production today don't paradoxically make future crashes in production more likely tomorrow. But we also need resilient local economies because their resilience can be a major factor that reduces their dependence on centrally distributed welfare.

The key characteristics of resilient systems are important here:[57]

- They are diverse, with a great variety of scale, function and survival strategies.
- They are not too closely integrated around a small number of concentrated organisms, whose failure could bring the whole system down.
- They exhibit duplication and redundancy so that some parts of the system can quickly compensate for problems in other parts.

A modern, efficient economic supply chain, such as the automotive industry, is dominated by a number of very large manufacturers which are not particularly diverse in their scale, ownership structures, technology or business models. They have driven out duplication and redundancy (such as holding stocks) to reduce costs. The Japanese earthquake and tsunami of March 2011 contributed to a dramatic decline in Japanese car production as might be expected. But it also disrupted car production globally as European and US plants reliant on a small number of preferred Japanese suppliers of parts were unable to compensate by increasing supplies from elsewhere, leading in some cases to temporary idling of production in non-Japanese plants.[58]

The logic of pursuing efficiency and large-scale concentration of production runs counter to the logic of building economic resilience. We must strive for balance.

This approach works with the grain of advances in technology. Revolutions including 3D printing and local shared production facilities, such as Fab Labs, combined with the rise of the peer-to-peer economy, pose a serious challenge to the need for large-scale centralised production.[59] If you can make things cheaply and easily in small batches, then the old economics of centralised economies of scale no longer apply in quite the same way. The falling cost of small-scale production makes bespoke, personalised products and services increasingly possible.[60]

What this means in practice is that we need to be able to produce goods and services at an appropriate scale to support balanced, diverse local and regional economies. It means reducing reliance on fossil fuels from transport. It requires investment in social as well as financial capital, which aims to address poverty and inequalities (of income, wealth, time, access and control over productive resources, and carbon). Above all, it requires us to recognise the value to be gained from allowing thousands of diverse local flowers to bloom, and perhaps intervening to prevent large, powerful and apparently more efficient international operations from overwhelming them.

Making the most of local economies

On the face of it, mainstream economic theory gives us good cause to treat attempts to help local economies with suspicion. But, dig a little deeper, and there are sound economic reasons to intervene to correct market failures that manifest in particular at a local level – perhaps where they are less obvious to national policymakers. Drawing on modern complexity science and systems thinking provides more theoretical underpinnings for applying economic and policy instruments to create more space for local economies to prosper. We need to provide more local choice while avoiding protecting less effective businesses, avoiding tit-for-tat retaliation where everywhere just employs their own workforce. The solution may be to develop Small Business Zones where some kind of privileging is possible, and where proper evaluation can be done (see Chapter 5 below).

This certainly does not mean imposing hard geographical boundaries or barriers to trade. It is less about borders and more about appropriate scale and diversity. We need to think about the nations' resources, not as homogenous masses of labour, capital and natural endowments, but as a conglomeration of bundles of local resources. Where these resources are persistently being under-used, we have a duty to act and – when we act – we have the chance to improve the productivity of the national economy as a whole.

**

Externalities, distorted competition, immobile labour and economic resilience are reasons why mainstream economics policy-makers need to look again at ultra-local approaches – and why their colleagues in cities and towns are beginning to do so: because it is no longer effective to allow the economy to remain unbalanced. Not just between sectors – but within every area and region, between the fast-moving and the sluggish and dependent. In the end, the argument comes down to practicalities – are there effective local levers which can be pulled to make a difference, using local resources to soak up unused capacity? Because market failure is an indication of economic opportunity.

The question then is whether, if the market is failing to recognise an opportunity at the appropriate time, some local intervention could make things happen better and faster. This may not always be about investment – which is available in other places – but can be about shaping the institutions we need to bring actors together to create mutual benefit. When it is hard for natural competitors, whether they are people, companies or local authorities, to work together to grasp the opportunity, there is a need for accessible institutions which can help them to remove the barriers to success.

In researching this book, we also talked to advocates and economists in the USA who are beginning to use the concepts and techniques of development economics to tackle the ultra-local problem. What they have shown us is that:

- Nobody wants to live in an insular, defensive, even xenophobic, local economy. That is no solution.
- Strictly speaking, this is not an ultra-local approach – it is an ultra-*small* one. It is about shaping the right local institutions to encourage new enterprises.
- This means creating, as an explicit objective, more

economic diversity and choice at local level – as well as national level – aware that consumers may use the extra money they save (brought by greater local competition) by trading more. Strictly speaking, protectionism limits choice – the objective here is to extend it.

5.   What should we do?

Outline of what this means in practice: how to support the development of local economies in disadvantaged areas, including new forms of measurement, developing micro-providers, a new local banking sector, Small Business Zones and secondary currency systems. The Treasury should provide a structure to co-ordinate this agenda at national level, and the Government should set as an objective that half of all business investment should go to the SME sector where half the profits are actually made.

Various early twentieth century business magnates are credited with the famous maxim that half of what they spent on advertising was wasted, but they didn't know which half. That is the difficulty of soaking up spare capacity in disadvantaged places, and by solving particular local market failures, just by pulling levers in Whitehall. It means that a great deal of the success will be wasted in inflationary growth in wealthy areas.

The reward for targeting resources more precisely, where they will be most effective, is that it would reduce the costs of welfare to central government. It would do so even though the resources might seem like they could be better spent elsewhere if they were measured by GVA alone. It might also be a way of adding to national prosperity as a whole and, by doing so, reducing the deficit. That is what happens when there are market failures at local level: it means the national economy is not working as efficiently as it could.

The heart of this issue – how cities and towns can tackle local market failure efficiently and cost effectively – is about encouraging and enabling enterprise. This can transcend traditional political boundaries. It may pit heterodox or development economics against mainstream economic policy, or localisers against centralisers – but otherwise it is a pragmatic business of finding successful policy levers that work. The only important question is: can new enterprises be developed in a targeted way to soak up spare capacity locally – and can this happen without creating unnatural boundaries that undermine people's choices and their ability to improve their lot?

Of course, it may be that this is just not possible, but experience in other countries suggests otherwise – and especially in Germany and the USA where the cities tend to work together to achieve it. Therefore it seems sensible to test out UK approaches along similar lines. Again, the only important question is whether it works.

There are the traditional justifications of economies of scale, which might still justify acting at national level alone, but these are dwindling: long-term energy price rises, the shift from the primacy of goods to services and the inefficiencies of global distribution systems, are all reasons why we need to take another look at the economics of place.

In which case, what would it mean in the UK? There is a range of ways in which ultra-local economics is creeping into the mainstream, via the Regional Growth Fund and the more innovative City Deals, many of which involve developing SMEs or local energy. But we are in the early stages, we lack the experience to really make this agenda effective yet. We still suffer from the reluctance to look at local economies, and the money that flows around them, at a very granular level. Most of all we lack the institutions capable of working with smaller players – certainly the banks have been unable to, and seem unlikely to be able to in the same way.

So when our cities extract extra powers from Whitehall – as they are now doing – what should they use them for? How can they learn from the success of devolved administrations like Germany? And what should they ask for from central government as part of the settlement?

Measurement tools

The argument for a better system of measuring economic success is clear from the Treasury's own far-sighted *Green Book*. Although this is nodded to in public, in practice, it is largely ignored. GVA has its role, but we need a range of other measurement techniques to inform it.

The new measurement toolbox will also require techniques for making the money flowing around a local economy more visible. Local economic development managers need to see where it is going more clearly, and the extent to which it is flowing to communities without enough money circulating in them – and where new enterprise could profitably intervene. Crucially, we need to help local authorities with the data they need to identify potential companies that could scale up successfully, as recommended by the recent *Scale Up* report, suggesting that the task is much more effective, and much less expensive, if it is done by local leaders in collaboration with universities.[61]

We propose that the Government holds a formal review on parallel measurement systems for economic development, which allows policies and potential projects to be evaluated on a wider basis than GVA – and that one measure, or a basket of measurements, should be adopted in parallel to GVA for all projects. This is most relevant to the way that LEPs measure their success – at the moment they are focused on improving national GVA, when it would instead make sense to bind them more closely to the objective of localising prosperity in their area.

Data about local money flows

Even more fundamental is the need to foster an interest in the granular detail of where money flows through city, regional or local economies. This is what lay behind the successful development of micro-enterprises in Italy's Emilia-Romagna area, after a very careful mapping of the regional economy, just as it was done to replicate that success in Quebec (see page 15). The tools for finding this data are increasingly available and we should use them, especially thanks to the new transparency of bank lending data down to postal district level.

Local enterprise and ownership

We hear less these days about 're-balancing' the economy, though the argument was set out coherently in 2009 by George Osborne that the UK economy had become too dependent on financial services, public spending and property.[62] That remains true, and what inhibits the shift we need is the old idea that no re-balancing is ever additional. As we argued above, this will tend to leave some cities more dependent on central welfare than they need to be. The City Growth Commission came to similar conclusions.[63]

Even if there is no hope of additional prosperity – because all growth is simply moved elsewhere – mainstream policy-makers accept that there may still be good reasons for moving it: the shift to a different place offers opportunity for improvement. It might build resilience in one place, but be creamed off in excess profits somewhere else.

The implication of this is that there are opportunities to grow the local supply side, along the lines set out by Bruce Katz and others, emphasising the creativity that becomes possible in urban clusters.[64] The City Growth Commission emphasised the importance of home-grown public service providers, as innovators and local earners, and this is the same direction taken by Quebec in the 1990s (see previous page).

Developing micro-enterprises

Nottinghamshire County Council pioneered a successful strategy through Community Catalysts, where they seconded an entrepreneurial individual whose task was to encourage new providers and micro-providers in the social care market to innovate with new ways of organising services and therefore increase employment of local people.[65] Based on Nottinghamshire County Council figures, it might be reasonable to expect each local scheme to enable 40 to 45 new providers to enter the market over a two year period (the scheme in Nottinghamshire led to 43 new 'micro providers' being set up in the social care market alone). This is a potential way forward for the paradox of Bradford (see page 7), where the talented and experienced women who have given up careers to look after children might welcome part-time employment running childcare co-ops – and would, in all probability, develop new ideas once people began meeting each other regularly.

But to achieve this, we need institutions which are set up at local level to offer the right help and support to encourage new entrepreneurs. The experience with Business Link was that it was too distant and too virtual to be of much use in the target market. Like BizFizz, the enterprise 'coaching' programme, local institutions need to be able to link people with ideas to local networks of support.[66] Plymouth City Council is one of the leaders on this issue, and has developed the Growth Acceleration Investment Network as part of their successful City Deal bid.[67]

Linking up high-growth companies locally

The traditional role of central government has been to offer to finance selected infrastructure projects which will, arguably, encourage external investment or help speed access to outside markets by the investors. The trouble with this approach is that it also shifts the focus away from home-grown solutions towards fitting proposals to national rules. It wastes time in gaming and competition and discourages places from looking at the resources that are already available to them. City Deals have begun to tackle this particular conundrum, but there remains more than an element of supplication from local to central, which may undermine objectives and certainly blunts ambition.

Most of the old RDAs used to have strategies to support 'high growth' start-ups, and there are various schemes at the Department for Business, Innovation and Skills (BIS), like the Growth Accelerator Programme, but most evidence suggests that these start-ups are actually quite unlike each other. And it is hard to tailor support for so diverse a phenomenon from Whitehall – let alone manage the financing when there is so little information about context.[68]

Seeking out the opportunities

If we agree that struggling local economies need to use their own resources more efficiently, then it makes sense to look at the biggest leaks in those economies. It makes no sense for cities to stay unconcerned about the way money flows around their local economy. They will have to work out how to diversify and to match unmet local needs with wasted local resources. This need not mean 'picking winners' any more than it means supporting losers, but it does require a more hands-on awareness of what local businesses need, how to develop the supply chains and how to use local procurement budgets more effectively to meet a wider range of local needs. This argument is won at national level – Vince Cable has presided over a new industrial strategy – but it has not yet been won at regional or local level.

Any measure must not imply absolute boundaries, but it should facilitate struggling areas to innovate in order to make their own economies more effective – and without the threat of wealthy areas hitting back. The Social Value Act already makes this possible, but its use depends on a much greater awareness of unmet needs and possible local markets. The Evergreen Project in Cleveland, Ohio, has pioneered a way for hospitals and universities to use their local procurement to shape a new generation of mutual social enterprises to meet local needs, improve health and training and revitalise employability.[69]

Small Enterprise Zones

As outlined previously, one tentative way forward would be for BIS and the Treasury to pilot Small Enterprise Zones, which have the power to innovate, and can direct public spending more effectively in the local economy. This might help to solve local market failure – and do so without damaging the quality and cost of local services – but on the understanding that this will not spread beyond the poorest areas.

Localising ownership

If the objective is to maximise local choice for struggling local economies, then it makes sense to provide choices

– especially in energy – which give people continuing ownership rights. Evidence from Germany and Denmark on how to forge social-public partnerships is impressive.[70]

Over the last 30 years in Denmark local farmers, local authorities and small businesses have developed co-operative energy solutions at scale, now accounting for some 40 per cent of ownership in the energy market, either municipally or co-operatively owned. In Germany the renewable energy market is now over 50 per cent owned by democratic bodies and citizens. This could be important for the future, given that direct shareholder ownership has continued to decline for decades. It could also put the rewards of investment back into struggling areas.

This implies that the Department of Energy and Climate Change (DECC) needs to set out a model for co-operation between local authorities and community energy organisations, so that local authorities increasingly become energy catalysts – as cities have done so successfully in Sweden, Denmark, Germany and Canada – providing some of the necessary skills to the community organisations. It should also mean giving communities the chance to invest in local energy. The objective must be community-led projects offering shares for 100 per cent local ownership, but owning some local shares in commercial developments is also helpful, like those offered by Falck Renewables.

Local finance and money

In order for struggling areas to regenerate, they will need to be able to access the finance they need to invest in business opportunities and improved infrastructure. Yet in many cases, as we know, this much needed finance is not forthcoming, in part because lenders don't have the local knowledge, but also because business prospects in a disadvantaged area may not seem good from a London or regional headquarters perspective.

There is a vicious cycle at work here. Lenders will not lend because the local economy is weak and the local economy is weak because lenders will not lend. A co-ordinating hand is required to break this vicious cycle and turn it into a virtuous one. Otherwise, the deposits from poorer areas – and the interest payments – will tend to flow back to institutions, which will tend to redirect it to the wealthiest areas. It is an unseen double disadvantage for those struggling places.

There are downsides to relying too much on local savings for local investment. It could make poorer communities more, rather than less, vulnerable, but this doesn't imply that all investment should be external, or that local savings should never be used as a local investment resource. It does imply that neither should be exclusive. And, at the moment, those institutions which can take an informed view of a local economy barely exist.

New local banking sector

One way the Government can break this logjam is to co-ordinate with the big banks so that they provide the money, and expertise, to shape a new local banking sector, linked to institutions providing mutual business advice and support. This money would be forthcoming in lieu of the money the big banks are unable to lend to SMEs because they lack the information they need, and should be related to their geographical lending data.[71] It could also come from fines levied by the Financial Conduct Authority.

The new mezzo level

One of the lessons of the ultra-micro – or ultra-small – approach is that the institutions that are intended to support small enterprise are too big to be effective. Paradoxically, providing micro institutions at local level may not be enough, because they are too isolated and vulnerable to do the job effectively. So there needs to be two new layers – local institutions capable of shaping economies on a smaller basis, from CDFIs (Community Development Finance Institutions) to enterprise centres, but also a new *mezzo* level – between macro and micro –where these institutions are federated to share risk and support. That is certainly the lesson of the local stakeholder banks in many countries which collaborate in networks to share risk, knowhow, technical skills and some back office functions.[72]

This appears also to be the pattern for the emerging 'sharing' economy. There are platforms made available at mezzo- and macro-level, which can then be adapted for use at local level. This is relevant to new financial institutions as well as to other kinds of sharing platforms, like those mutual organisations developed by companies like Best Western or the Freelancers Union of New York. It is relevant also to the new generation of social care mutuals and childcare mutuals which have been such a success in Scandinavia and North America.

New investment institutions

If half of the employment and value added comes from small business, yet they get less than half the benefit from the nation's investment, that is in itself a capital market failure which must be addressed – not so much in the name of equity, but in the name of economic efficiency. It means that the potentially profitable companies are not getting the capital they need because the big financial institutions are bad at assessing risk in this sector.

Again, the debate in the USA has gone some way ahead of the equivalent debate in the UK. This capital markets imbalance was addressed by the US Jobs Act 2012, known colloquially as the Jump-Start Business Act. It provided a means by which anybody with $2,000 could invest it in a small business, if it was done through an approved website. In practice the federal regulators have failed to implement the law and so similar arrangements have begun to emerge at the level of individual states.

The legal restrictions on individuals investing in small companies are different in the USA, and in some ways tougher than they are here. But, even so, we don't have the institutions which make it possible on a major scale, though peer-to-peer lending (P2P), backed by the British Business Bank is beginning to do so. The basic capital market failure remains and, thanks to new regulations on bank lending – which impact much harder on small banks than on the big ones they were designed for – the situation is likely to get worse.

In 1998, the Canadian province of Nova Scotia passed the Community Economic Development Investment Funds (CEDIF) Act, which laid out a simple process by which unaccredited investors could pool money and provide loans to local businesses. Residents of Nova Scotia are allowed to place their tax-deferred retirement savings into these funds. Since then, this province of a million people has seen the creation of nearly 50 funds, most of them focused on helping farmers and local food businesses.

We also need to experiment with:

- Local pension funds, sharing risk between them across the UK, but investing in housing finance and other safe infrastructure investments.
- Local exchanges that allow the funds to buy and sell bonds and shares from smaller businesses (illiquid securities are potentially worthless) – which will depend on there being enough local securities to trade.
- Innovative forms of pre-selling to fund new businesses or the expansion of old ones. Restaurants like Clare's, in Hardwick, Vermont, used the pre-purchase of a package of meals to create a restaurant, supported by an infrastructure which made this form of finance possible (in this case, Credibles, which allows businesses to take out a line of credit with their customer base, instead of going to the bank).[73]

New development bank

It also makes sense that the Government should merge the various Whitehall arms currently providing development finance, and turn it into a development bank with a charter that makes it answerable to Parliament. The Government is now operating a development bank by default, through the funding and loan arrangements in a number of different government departments, from the Regional Growth Fund to Innovate UK (previously the Technology Strategy Board). The difficulty is that none of them are good at reaching effective, smaller players. Merging these together will give them the opportunity to learn independently of the Government.

If KfW in Germany has the privilege of making wholesale loans below market prices, and the UK can do the same for big banks under Funding for Lending, these schemes should be extended in the UK to local institutions with some track record at lending effectively to small businesses. The UK has the beginnings of a community development banking infrastructure, and we should now use this infrastructure to lend on 'patient capital', as they do so successfully in Germany and the USA.

New property lending

We also need providers of mortgage finance via a new generation of regional building societies, which can retain some interest in the struggling areas. Local authorities provided staff mortgages until the 1970s, but this has dwindled too. The Government also needs to investigate why it appears to be so difficult for new entrants to the building society market – and new building societies will need protection from being forced into becoming banks.

These peculiarities need to be looked at again, along with other measures to tackle the destructive rises in land values, which have been tackled very widely across North America using community land trusts (CLTs). These divide the ownership of the buildings from the ownership of the underlying land, which allows regions to keep the homes affordable.

Secondary money systems

These systems offer a route to address local imbalances of market power. Small traders can't compete with the marketing muscle of large corporations, but by participating in local currency schemes they can offer a kind of pooled customer loyalty scheme, together with a means of increasing their visibility to customers. They can also stimulate smaller local providers by looking for opportunities to spend their local currency further down their supply chain.

The recent Bank of England report on complementary currencies suggests that there might be occasions when secondary currencies could be useful in reaching the parts of a local economy, and encouraging enterprise, in a way that other more expensive forms of regeneration are unable to, because specific money systems can target specific problems.[74]

This is particularly the case when creating very low cost local credit that does not rely on banks, or any other external providers, but is delivered by participating businesses to one another in mutual credit schemes. The Swiss Wirtschaftsring, or WIR, has been operating such a scheme successfully since 1934, and new versions are springing up such as the SoNantes system in Brittany.[75] Peer-to-peer money systems are potentially a market-based solution to achieving the same regeneration objectives at lower costs than Whitehall could manage. The difficulty is that their regulatory position is ambiguous, especially on continental Europe where central banks are particularly nervous of them: they need enabling regulation that opens up the possibilities for experiment and innovation. It makes sense that within Europe the Bank of England should take the lead in regulating secondary money systems, and organising research into their best practice.

Two actions for Government

This book has set out a series of reasons why mainstream economic policy-makers need to focus at a more granular level, and how all places, urban and rural can justify their interest in this area, using local pride as a major asset and source of energy to regenerate their most impoverished areas. It makes two important proposals:

As a rule of thumb, we believe the Government should aim for at least half the business investment in the UK going into the profitable half of the economy which currently gets the least. If SMEs earn 51 per cent of the profits in the UK (see page 52), they should to get half the private sector investment too. If they are not doing so, then we need to provide the intermediaries and institutions which could make this possible. In the interim, **the Government needs to track these numbers regularly – comparing profitability and investment by size of business – and to report on them.**

Also the structures of UK policy-making need to reflect the importance of ultra-local economic policy. **The Treasury needs to set up an ultra-local policy and delivery unit,** learning the lessons from the What Works Centre for Local Economics, and fulfilling the following tasks:

- Advising ministers on the barriers to local economic development, and what we call people-powered prosperity, in all the cities and regions of the UK – and on what institutions are needed locally and nationally to achieve it.
- Reporting on local economic progress and lessons, and capturing progress in more appropriate measures.
- Co-ordinating policy across government departments to achieve these objectives.

The approach set out here is one which uses a vital, forgotten economic resource: local pride. Mainstream economics has never really understood local pride as a factor, but cities are increasingly aware of how powerful it can be – if the local institutions are in place, and if the techniques are available to tackle local market failure. That is prosperity that depends on local ingenuity, driven by local people, based on their growing awareness of the resources that are lying unused in their very midst. That is People-Powered Prosperity.

Conclusions summary

This report has two clear proposals. The first is about investment in small business, which now earns 51 per cent of value added in the UK economy. These businesses should therefore be getting a similar proportion of the business investment available in the UK. If they are not doing so, then it is a serious market failure and we need to provide the intermediaries and institutions which could make this possible.

In the interim, the Government needs to track these numbers regularly – comparing profitability and investment by size of business – and report on them.

The second proposal relates to the development of a body pf practical knowledge about ultra-local economic solutions. The Treasury needs to set up an ultra-local policy and delivery unit, learning the lessons from the What Works Centre for Local Economics, and the experience of local authorities in urban and rural areas, which are succeeding in developing working solutions to their economic difficulties.

⊟ Evidence and note on further reading

Relevant research findings are referenced where they support the various claims in this book, but also we recommend the evidence review by Localise West Midlands (Morris, J.; Cobbing, P.; Leach, K and Conaty, P. (2013), *Mainstreaming Community Economic Development*, Birmingham: Localise West Midlands).[76]

⊕ Acknowledgements

We are tremendously grateful to the staff and trustees of the Friends Provident Foundation, without whom this book would not have been possible, and particularly to Andrew Thompson and Sue Scott for all their help and advice. The Foundation has carved a pioneering path in the development of resilient economic systems and deserves the gratitude of the emerging sector for their important role. We would also like to thank Nick Edmonds, who provided economic advice throughout the project, though he does not necessarily endorse all our conclusions, and Michael Shuman and Nigel Jump who read through the whole manuscript and made suggestions. We would like to thank the team who ran the project, including Sarah Burns, Angie Greenham and Lindsay Mackie, and all those involved in the production of *People Powered Prosperity*. Finally, we would like to thank all those who gave us advice via interviews, round tables or in some other way. The names of all our interviewees are listed at the end of this book. Their inclusion on the list doesn't imply that they agree with us, but they all helped develop our thinking and gave their time and thoughts generously. We couldn't have done it without them.

New Weather team
David Boyle
Sarah Burns
Nick Edmonds
Tony Greenham
Lindsay Mackie

Advisory panel
Pat Conaty, Co-operatives UK
Ben Hughes, Community Development Finance Association
Rachel Laurence, New Economics Foundation
Karen Leach, Localise West Midlands
Peter Lipman, Sustrans
Neil McInroy, Centre for Local Economic Strategies
Frances Northrop, Transition Towns RE-economy Programme
Fiona Ward, Transition Towns

Interviewees
None of these individuals or their institutions should be regarded as responsible for any of the views expressed here

Attendees at two round tables:
  Plymouth Business School
  HM Treasury
Professor Steven Brand, Plymouth University
Diane Coyle, Manchester University
Edward Twiddy, Atombank
John Fullerton, Capital Institute (New York)
Nigel Jump, Strategic Economics Ltd
Tim Leunig, Department for Education

ACKNOWLEDGEMENTS

Ben Lucas, Royal Society of Arts
Professor Marguerite Mendell, Concordia University
Professor Jim O'Neill, City Growth Commission
Professor Henry Overman, What Works Centre for Local Economics
Lord Shipley
Neil Smith, Plymouth Business School
Michael Shuman, Business Alliance for Local Living Economies (California)
Geoff Tily, TUC

❂ Notes

1   Priestley, J. B. (1977), *English Journey,* London: Penguin Books, 156.
2   Greenhalf, J. (2013), 'Building a picture of poverty in Bradford',
    Bradford Telegraph & Argus, 1 Aug.
3   Leunig, T. and Swaffield, J. (2008), *Cities Unlimited,* London: Policy
    Exchange.
4   See Paul Seabright's critique of micro-economics teaching: http://
    www.project-syndicate.org/commentary/
    paul-seabright-criticizes-the-poverty-of-the-undergraduate-
    microeconomics-curriculum
5   http://www.barrowcadbury.org.uk/wp-content/uploads/2013/02/
    MCED-final-report-LWM-Jan-2013.pdf
6   http://sec.oise.utoronto.ca/english/project_outputs/
    project33_February09Report.pdf
7   Mendell, M. and Neantam, N. (2008), *The Social Economy in Quebec:
    Towards a New Political Economy,* Concordia University.
8   Bendle, S. and Conaty, P. (2014), 'In Trust', *Fabian Review,* Volume
    126, No 2, Summer.
9   de Castro, O. et al (2010), *Monitoring the Impact of an Innovative
    Community Banking Network in Brazil,* Instituto Palmas, Brazil;
    Joaquim de Melo Neto, J. (2002), *Community Banks Microcredit: The
    case of Brazil,* Las Palmas: Instituto Banco Palmas; and Tendler, J.
    (2001), *Transforming Local Economies: Lessons from the Northeast
    Brazilian Experience,* Massachusetts Institute of Technology/Bank of
    Northeast.

[10] http://www.barrowcadbury.org.uk/wp-content/uploads/2013/02/MCED-final-report-LWM-Jan-2013.pdf

[11] Mundell, R. A. (1961), 'A Theory of Optimal Currency Zones', *American Economic Review*, 54 (4), 657–665.

[12] Michael Shuman, in conversation with the authors, 27 Oct 2014.

[13] Rupasingha, A. (2013), *Locally Owned: Do Local Business Ownership and Size Matter for Local Economic Well-being?*, Federal Reserve Bank of Atlanta, discussion paper 1-13.

[14] Jacobs, J. (1985), *Cities and the Wealth of Nations*, New York: Random House.

[15] Kim, S. (1998), 'Regions, Resources, and Economic Geography: Sources of U.S. Regional Comparative Advantage, 1880–1987', *Regional Science and Urban Economics*. Also available as NBER working paper #6322 (1998). See also Krugman, P. (2011), New Economic Geography, now middle-aged', *Regional Studies*, Vol. 45.1, pp. 1–7, Jan.

[16] http://mises.org/library/jane-jacobs-anti-planner

[17] Jacobs, J. (1969), *The Economy of Cities,* New York: Vintage, 161.

[18] IFF Research (2012), *Welfare to Self Employment*, London: BIS, 6ff.

[19] http://www.inc.com/magazine/19960701/1725.html

[20] For example, one study in a Chicago neighbourhood showed that a dollar spent at a local restaurant yielded a 25 per cent greater economic multiplier effect than at a chain restaurant. Matt Cunningham and Dan Houston (2004), *The Andersonville Study of Retail Economics*, Chicago: Civic Economics.

[21] In economics the Lump of Labour Fallacy is used to describe the notion that there is a fixed amount of work to be done that can be shared out it different ways. In fact, any change in the distribution

of work amongst the population is likely to have an impact on the total amount of work done by the population.

[22] The argument that Uber is growing the market for taxis is set out in a detailed blog post by Uber board member Bill Gurley: http://abovethecrowd.com/2014/07/11/how-to-miss-by-a-mile-an-alternative-look-at-ubers-potential-market-size/

[23] City Growth Commission (2014), *Unleashing Metro Growth*, London: Royal Society of Arts.

[24] City Growth Commission (2014), op cit.

[25] Lee, N. et al (2013). *Cities, Growth and Poverty: a Review of the Evidence*, Joseph Rowntree Foundation, York.

[26] Meade, D. S. (2010), 'Why Real Value Added is Not my Favourite Concept', *Studies in Russian Economic Development*, Vol 21, 3. 249-262.

[27] It also fails to tell us about a range of other issues – like the patter of beneficial ownership, the geographical spread of the jobs created, the multiplier effects of the spending that results, and much more besides.

[28] https://www.gov.uk/government/uploads/system/uploads/attachment_data/file/220541/green_book_complete.pdf

[29] http://www.ons.gov.uk/ons/rel/regional-trends/regional-economic-analysis/gva-for-local-enterprise-partnerships/art-lep-gva.html

[30] https://www.london.gov.uk/priorities/business-economy/working-in-partnership/london-enterprise-panel/strategic-focus/economic-development-plan

[31] Volterra Partners (2014), *Investing in City Regions: The Case for Long-term Investment in Transport*, London.

[32] Henry, N. et al (2013), *An Economic Impact Tool for the Community*

Finance Industry, Centre for Economics and Society, CDFA, London.

[33] https://www.gov.uk/government/uploads/system/uploads/attachment_data/file/220541/green_book_complete.pdf

[34] See for example: https://www.youtube.com/watch?feature=player_embedded&v=ktjvoTwmsko

[35] Keynes, J.M. (1933), 'National Self-Sufficiency', *Yale Review* 22, 769.

[36] There have been various attempts to do so, notably in Michael Danson's micro studies, and much less precise attempts using LM3 (https://www.lm3online.com/about).

[37] Glaeser, E.L. and Kerr, W. (2010), 'The Secret to Job Growth: Think Small', *Harvard Business Review*, July.

[38] Fleming, D.A. and Goetz, S.J. (2011), 'Does Local Firm Ownership Matter?', *Economic Development Quarterly*, August, vol. 25, (3), 277-281.

[39] See Benhabib, J. & Farmer, R.E.A. (1998) *Indeterminacy and Sunspots in Macroeconomics*, Journal of Economic Theory, 81, 1-6; see also Woodford, M. (1990), 'Learning to Believe in Sunspots', *Econometrica*, Vol 58, No 2 (Mar), 277-307.

[40] http://pwc.blogs.com/northern-ireland/2014/08/uks-sharing-economy-could-be-worth-9-billion-a-year-by-2025.html

[41] Banerjee, A. and Duflo, E. (2012), *Poor Economics*, London: Penguin Books, 163.

[42] Shuman, M. (2011), *Local Dollars, Local Sense*, White River Junction: Chelsea Green, 14ff.

[43] Department of Energy and Climate Change (2014) *Community Energy Strategy: Full Report*, London.

[44] For more information, see: Grossman, S. J and Stiglitz, J. E. (1978), 'On the Impossibility of Informationally Efficient Markets', *American Economic Review*, June; see also Townsend, R.M. (1979),

'Optimal Contracts and Competitive Markets with Costly State Verification', *Journal of Economic Theory*, Elsevier, vol 21(2).

[45] See Williams, G. (2011), *Slow Finance: Why Investment Miles Matter*, London: Bloomsbury.

[46] http://www.fsb.org.uk/stats

[47] OECD (2009), *Structural and Demographic Business Statistics*, Paris: OECD, 353.

[48] Both the modern incarnations of the Liberal Democrat and Conservative Parties and the international magazine *The Economist*, can trace their roots to the political mobilisation of the Anti-Corn Law League against protectionism in the mid 1800s.

[49] Ricardo, D. (1821), *On the Principles of Political Economy and Taxation,* Library of Economics and Liberty. Retrieved November 18, 2014 from the World Wide Web: http://www.econlib.org/library/Ricardo/ricP2a.html

[50] Professor Richard Werner sets out a comprehensive and amusing list of the activities and organisations that would not exist under conditions of perfect information including insurance, advertising, consultancy, legal advice, estate agents, economic forecasting, meetings, stockbroking, fund management and securitisation. See Werner, R.A. (2005), *New Paradigm in Macroeconomics*. Basingstoke: Palgrave Macmillan., pp. 20–24

[51] Naqvi, M. and Southgate, J. (2013), 'Banknotes, Local Currencies and Central Bank Objectives' in *Bank of England Quarterly Bulletin* 2013 Q4 pp 317-325. London: Bank of England.

[52] http://www.foodmanufacture.co.uk/Regulation/Food-firms-call-for-more-on-supermarket-abuse

[53] See detail about Northumbria at: file:///C:/Users/user/Downloads/358121K_SGE_flyer.pdf

[54] See for example: Lovins, A. and Lovins H. (1982), *Brittle Power*

[55] Greenham, T.; Cox, E. and Ryan-Collins, J. (2013), *Mapping Economic Resilience*, York: Friends Provident Foundation.

[56] http://www.economist.com/node/21541826

[57] For a good introduction to principles of resilience see Stockholm Resilience Centre (2014) *Applying Resilience Thinking: Seven principles for building resilience in social-ecological systems.* Stockholm: Stockholm Resilience Centre. Accessed on 10 Dec 2014 at http://www.stockholmresilience.org/download/18.10119fc11455d3c557d6928/1398150799790/SRC+Applying+Resilience+final.pdf

[58] http://www.go2uti.com/documents/10157/100902/TheLogisticsInstituteAsiaPacific-CombatingSupplyChainDisruptions-WhitePaper.pdf

[59] http://www.fablabsuk.co.uk/

[60] There is increasing anecdotal evidence that this is what groups of consumers are increasingly demanding, as the rise of Etsy and others implies: see Boyle, D. (2004), *Authenticity: Brands, Fakes, Spin and the Lust for Real Life*, London: HarperCollins Perennial.

[61] http://www.lse.ac.uk/publicEvents/pdf/2014-MT/20141118-ScaleUpManifestoPPTs.pdf

[62] http://www.rsablogs.org.uk/2009/education/osbornes-politics-of-austerity/

[63] City Growth Commission (2014), *Unleashing Metro Growth*, London: Royal Society of Arts.

[64] Katz, B. and Wagner, J. (2014), 'The Rise of Urban Innovation Districts', *Harvard Business Review*, Nov 12.

[65] http://www.communitycatalysts.co.uk/wp-content/uploads/2014/

08/Nottinghamshire-Micro-enterprise-Project-Final-Report-July-2014.pdf

[66] Boyle, D et al (2010), *Who's the Entrepreneur? The BizFizz Story*, London: New Economics Foundation.

[67] http://www.plymouth.gov.uk/gain

[68] Brown, R.; Mason, C. and Mawson, S. (2014), *Increasing 'The Vital 6 Percent': Designing Effective Public Policy to Support High Growth Firms*, Nesta Working Paper No. 14/01, London: Nesta, 6ff.

[69] http://evergreencooperatives.com/

[70] Lewis, M. and Conaty, P. (2012), *The Resilience Imperative: Co-operative Transitions to a Steady State Economy*, Vancouver: New Society Publishers, 61-4.

[71] Boyle (2014), op cit.

[72] Prieg, L. and Greenham, T. (2013), *Stakeholder Banks: Benefits of Banking Diversity*, New Economics Foundation, London.

[73] https://credibles.co/

[74] Naqvi, M. and Southgate, J. (2013), *'Banknotes, Local Currencies and Central Bank Objectives'*, London: Bank of England.

[75] Find out more about the WIR at http://community-currency.info/en/videos/learn-more/wir-bank-economic-cooperative/, and SoNantes at http://community-currency.info/en/currencies/sonantes/

[76] http://www.barrowcadbury.org.uk/wp-content/uploads/2013/02/MCED-final-report-LWM-Jan-2013.pdf